FEATS OF COURAGE

space∞

Business Leaders	Military Might
Engineering Wonders	Sports Superstitions
Extreme Survival	Unusual Jobs
Feats of Courage	Women in Combat
Hacking for Good	Wrongly Accused
Incredible Comebacks	

SADDLEBACK
EDUCATIONAL PUBLISHING
www.sdlback.com

Photo credits: page 6: Lilac Mountain/Shutterstock.com; pages 8/9: National Archives/Hulton Archive via Getty Images; page 10: Handout/Getty Images News via Getty Images; page 11: JNix/Shutterstock.com; page 12: MPI/Archive Photos via Getty Images; page 13: Michael Ochs Archive/Michael Ochs Archive via Getty Images; pages 14/15: Keystone Features/Hulton Archive via Getty Images; page 16: Win McNamee/Getty Images News via Getty Images; page 17: Everett Historical/Shutterstock.com; page 19: Hulton Archive/Hulton Archive via Getty Images; page 20: Fotosearch/Archive Photos via Getty Images; page 22: Nigel Waldron/Getty Images Entertainment via Getty Images; page 25: Osugi/Shutterstock.com; page 26: Patrick Christain/Hulton Archive via Getty Images; page 27: Keystone/Hulton Archive via Getty Images; page 28: Phil Pasquini/Shutterstock.com; page 29: Olga Popova/Shutterstock.com; pages 30/31: Hulton Archive/Hulton Archive via Getty Images; page 32: Everett Historical/Shutterstock.com; pages 36/37: Harry Scull Jr./Getty Images News via Getty Images; page 38: Chip Somodevilla/Getty Images News via Getty Images; page 39: Paul McKinnon/Shutterstock.com; pages 42/43: Leonard Zhukovsky/Shutterstock.com; page 44: Michael Graae/Getty Images News via Getty Images; page 45: Linh Pham/Getty Images News via Getty Images; pages 46/47: Lauren DeCicca/Getty Images News via Getty Images; page 48: Chris Jackson/Chris Jackson Collection via Getty Images; page 49: Lintao Zhang/Getty Images Entertainment via Getty Images; page 52: Jeff Swensen/Getty Images News via Getty Images

ISBN: 978-1-68021-747-6
eBook: 978-1-64598-053-7

Printed in Malaysia

27 26 25 24 23   3 4 5 6 7

TABLE OF CONTENTS

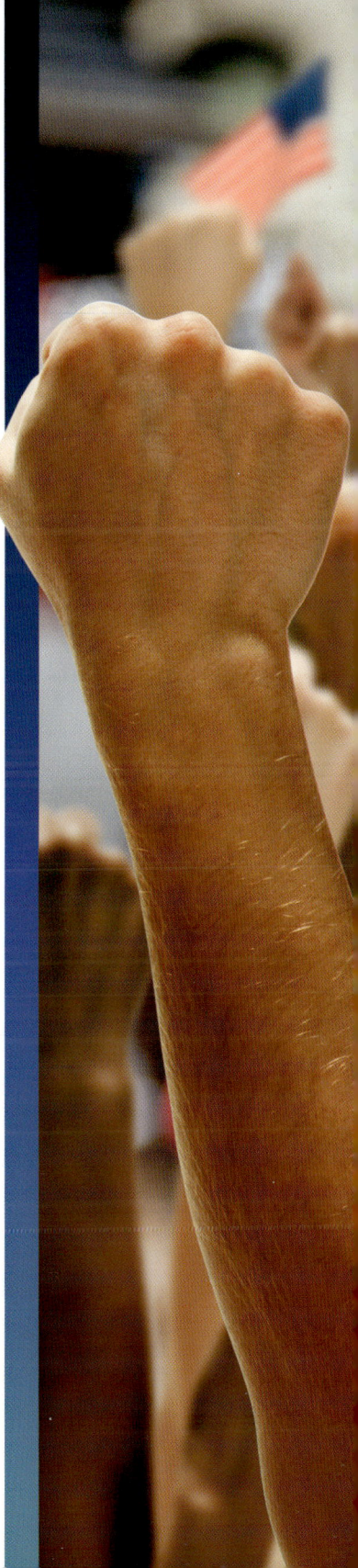

CHAPTER 1

HEROES AND COURAGE

What makes a hero? Some people say strength. Others say **empathy.** But many agree on one thing. All heroes need **courage.**

Courage helps people do things that scare them. Soldiers run into battle. Pilots fly into storms. A student raises her hand in class. All of them may feel fear. However, they push beyond the fear.

Heroes may be faced with danger and fear. Even still, they do great things. These heroic actions can be called feats.

A feat of courage can be small. It might help one person. Maybe it helps one animal. Small feats happen every day. Large feats are rare. Big, heroic actions can change a country. Some change the entire world.

People look up to heroes. They like to learn about them. Stories of courage are inspiring. Reading these stories can help readers be courageous too.

HERACLES THE PROTECTOR

People in ancient Greece loved hero stories. These tales are about 3,000 years old. One favorite hero was Heracles. In Rome, his name was Hercules.

The hero's father was a god named Zeus. His mother was a Greek woman. Heracles was kind and very strong. This strength let him battle many monsters.

Heracles went through many hardships. He had inner strength too. This made him an inspirational hero. The Greeks saw him as a protector.

CHAPTER 2
CIVIL RIGHTS

Slaves are people who work without pay. They are not free. Long ago, Americans had slaves. People were taken from Africa and sold. This ended in the 1800s.

After slavery, African Americans did not have equal rights. White people and African Americans were kept apart. There were separate schools. African Americans had to use different libraries too. This separation was called **segregation.** It was the law. Then, the Civil Rights Movement happened in the 1950s. Things began to change. African Americans stood up for their rights. Many people had courage.

CIVIL RIGHTS RALLY

It only took a moment for Rosa Parks to change the world. She was riding a bus. The driver told her to move. Her seat would go to a white man. Parks refused. This action was shocking. Rules were always obeyed. This woman was one of the first to break the rules. Police arrested her.

ROSA PARKS

THE BUS STOP
The Montgomery Bus Boycott

At the stop on this site on December 1, 1955, Mrs. Rosa Parks boarded the bus which would transport her name into history. Returning home after a long day working as a seamstress for Montgomery Fair department store, she refused the bus driver's order to give up her seat to boarding whites. Her arrest, conviction, and fine launched the Montgomery Bus Boycott. The Boycott began December 5, the day of Parks's trial, as a protest by African-Americans for unequal treatment they received on the bus line. Refusing to ride the buses, they maintained the Boycott until the U.S. Supreme Court ordered integration of public transportation one year later. Dr. Martin Luther King, Jr. led the Boycott, the beginning of the modern Civil Rights Movement.

SPONSORED BY ALPHA KAPPA ALPHA SORORITY, INCORPORATED DURING ITS CENTENNIAL SALUTE
ALABAMA HISTORICAL ASSOCIATION   2008

Parks's feat inspired others. Her courage ignited a fire in people. They began to fight for their rights. A bus **boycott** was started. It lasted more than a year. This got the country's attention. In 1956, the **Supreme Court** changed the rules. Anyone could sit in any bus seat. But the Civil Rights Movement had just begun.

In 1960, African Americans were still fighting for change. Ezell Blair Jr., David Richmond, Franklin McCain, and Joseph McNeil were students. They decided to **protest.** The students went to a lunch counter. Then they sat down. Only white people could sit there. Blair and his friends knew it was risky. Police could arrest them.

The young men would not leave. Other students joined them. Soon there were 300 people. Some were arrested. More came to take their place. Restaurants were forced to change their rules. It became law to serve whites and African Americans equally.

For many more years, the movement continued. There were more boycotts. People marched. They protested. Their fight was often met with violence. But it also led to change. New laws were made. The laws protected African Americans' right to equality.

MARTIN LUTHER KING JR.

Martin Luther King Jr. was a leader of the Civil Rights Movement. Many people did not like him. In 1958, a woman stabbed him. Police arrested him many times for protesting. But the hero had courage.

King did not believe in violence. Peace was his goal. The leader gave speeches and held boycotts. His actions inspired many people, including Rosa Parks.

King's work led to many changes. This included voting rights for African Americans. He won the Nobel Peace Prize. King was shot and killed in 1968. Every third Monday of January Americans celebrate Martin Luther King Jr. Day.

MARTIN LUTHER KING JR.

CHAPTER 3
WAR

War brings **tragedy.** Soldiers lose their lives. Citizens do too. There is much danger. When battles rage, heroes are made.

World War II lasted from 1939 to 1945. The Nazis were from Germany. They thought Germans were superior. Other people were hated, especially Jewish people.

Witold Pilecki was a soldier. With the Polish Army, he fought in the war. Pilecki became a spy. Then he did the unthinkable. He let the Nazis capture him. This action risked his life.

The man was taken to a camp for prisoners. There, he saw the Nazis. They were killing Jewish people. Most people did not know they were doing this. Because of Pilecki's work, news spread. Many countries decided to fight. In 1948, the brave man was killed for spying.

POLISH WORLD WAR II PILOTS

Desmond Doss was a U.S. soldier in World War II. Other soldiers bullied him. It was because he didn't carry a gun. Doss did not believe in fighting. Still, he wanted to serve. So Doss became a medic. During the war, he saved those bullies' lives.

In 1945, there was a battle. Japanese soldiers had large guns. They fired on the Americans. Many soldiers fell. Orders to retreat were given. Doss refused to leave. He ran alone onto the battlefield. There was nothing to protect him. All night, he pulled hurt people to safety. At least 50 lives were saved. President Truman gave Doss the Medal of Honor.

Kyle Carpenter also got a Medal of Honor. He was in Afghanistan in 2010. Enemies attacked. One threw a **grenade.** It landed near Carpenter and his friend. To protect his friend, the hero jumped on it. The blast hurt him badly. His right eye was lost. Many teeth were ruined. Bones were broken. About 40 surgeries were done. Carpenter had to leave the military. But he had saved his friend's life.

KYLE CARPENTER

SERGEANT STUBBY

Not all heroes are human. Sergeant Stubby was a dog who became a hero in World War I. In 1917, Stubby was a stray dog. Then he was adopted by an American soldier. The soldier took Stubby to war. They went to Europe. Stubby was in 17 battles.

Thanks to his excellent sense of smell, Stubby sniffed out hurt soldiers. He could also hear gunfire from far away and warn soldiers.

After the war, Stubby came home. Several U.S. presidents met him. The Humane Education Society gave him a medal. Stubby's story still inspires people. A movie was made about him in 2018, called *Sgt. Stubby: An American Hero.*

CHAPTER 4

WOMEN'S RIGHTS

Women have not always had equal rights. They have been barred from voting and driving cars. Sometimes they are paid less than men. This is true in the U.S. and across the world. Many people have fought for women's rights. These heroes have helped all women.

Mary Wollstonecraft was one of the first **feminists.** She lived in England in the late 1700s. People were shocked by her ideas. But she kept speaking up. Women were supposed to stay quiet. They were not allowed to go to school. Sometimes they had tutors.

Wollstonecraft was a writer. She wrote a popular book in 1788. Then she wrote an article. The article was **scandalous.** It said women should go to school. This would make them better people. School would also let them work skilled jobs. Her article was bold. But she wrote with passion. People began to listen.

MARY WOLLSTONECRAFT

In England in the late 1800s, women could not vote. Emmeline Pankhurst fought for this right. She was sent to prison. There, she and other women chose to go hungry. It was a hunger strike. This means not eating in protest. They hoped it would spur change.

EMMELINE PANKHURST

Pankhurst was an **activist.** Police arrested her several times. Also, she started important women's groups. The feminist traveled to other countries. Many people listened to her talk. Her feats inspired others. Finally, in 1918, women in England could vote. This **heroine**'s fight changed the world.

Malala Yousafzai was born in 1997 in Pakistan. Many girls are not allowed to go to school there. Laws forbid it. In 2012, Yousafzai wrote about it on her blog. She was 15. People wanted her to be quiet. A man shot her in the head. But the young activist lived. She wrote a book in 2013. Then she was given the Nobel Peace Prize. Her courage has been an inspiration to many.

MALALA YOUSAFZAI

HYSTERICAL STRENGTH

One woman lifts an entire car. A mother stands up to a tornado. These sound like urban legends. But they are true stories.

In 2012, Lauren Kornacki lifted a car that had fallen on her father. Kornacki gave him CPR. Her actions saved his life.

Also in 2012, there was a tornado. It hit Stephanie Decker's house. She had two young children. Decker threw herself over her kids. The tornado destroyed the house. But the mother held on. Both her legs were lost, but her children were not hurt.

Scientists think the human body is strong. In danger, people can use their full strength. It is called hysterical strength. This kind of strength let these women do incredible feats.

CHAPTER 5
RELIGIOUS FREEDOM

For many people, religion is important. Religion can help during hard times. It can also provide guidance in daily life. People have not always been free to practice religion. They had to fight for that freedom.

In 1536, William Tyndale was put to death. But he died a champion of religious freedom. Tyndale was a teacher. He worked at the University of Cambridge in England. At this time, only a few people could read the Bible. This is because it was written in Latin.

Tyndale thought all people should be able to read the Bible. So he **translated** it into English. By doing this, he broke a law. The teacher fled the country. Then he was betrayed. This betrayal led to Tyndale's arrest and death.

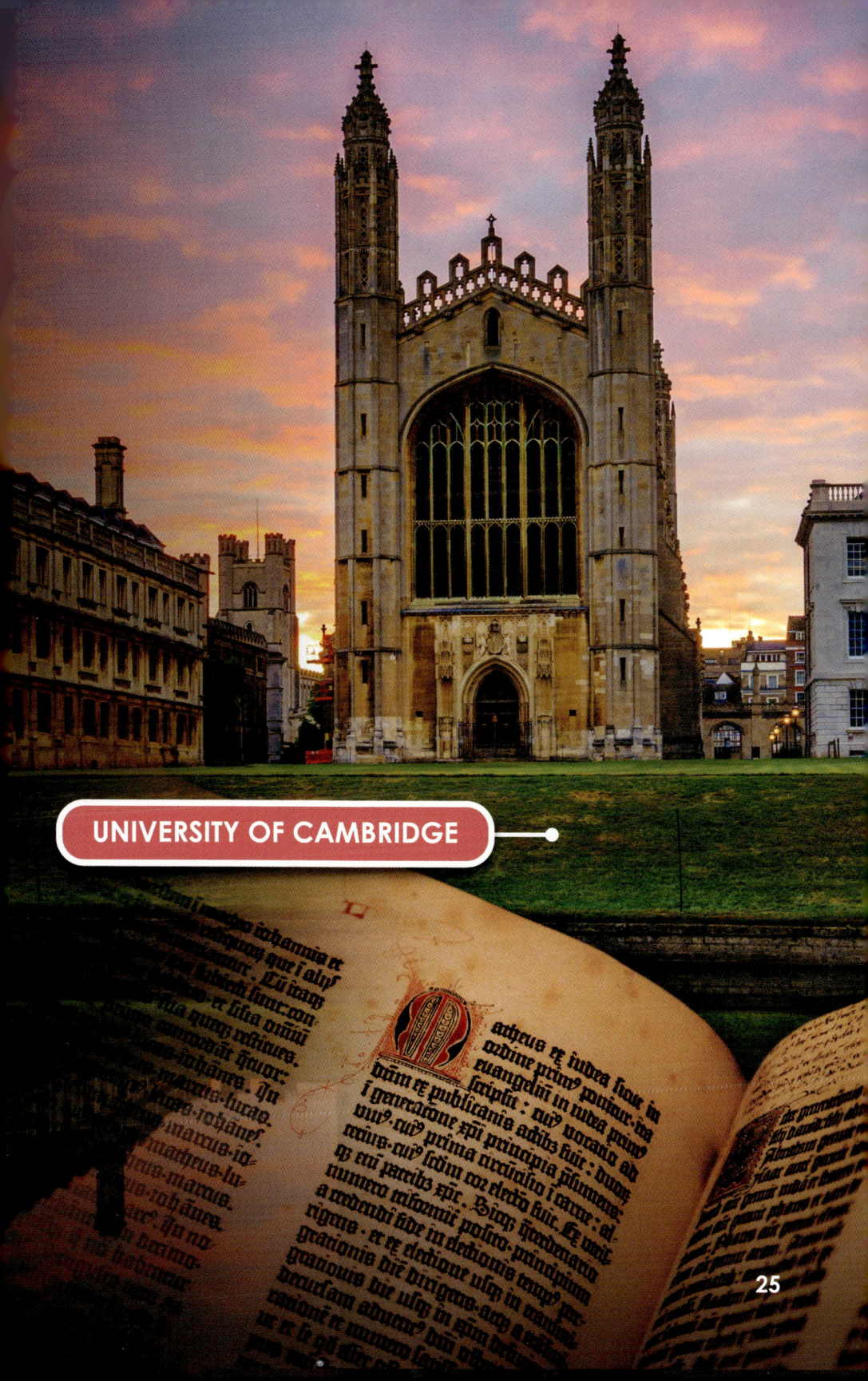

UNIVERSITY OF CAMBRIDGE

"Float like a butterfly. Sting like a bee." Muhammad Ali is famous for these words. He was talking about boxing. But he also spoke about religious freedom. In 1955, the Vietnam War started. The boxer was drafted in 1967. When drafted, a person has to become a soldier. Ali refused to join. His religion did not allow him to fight in wars. Because of this, he was banned from boxing.

VIETNAM

MUHAMMAD ALI

For three years, Ali could not participate in the sport he loved. But the athlete stood by his beliefs. Later, in 1971, the Supreme Court voted. Judges agreed with Ali. They said his religion meant he did not have to fight. Two years later, drafting was ended.

As a young girl, Ilhan Omar left Somalia. There was war there. Many people were being killed. Her family fled to the United States. They moved to Minnesota in 1997. Omar grew up a **minority.** Later, she went into politics.

In 2018, she was elected to the U.S. House of Representatives. She is one of the first American Muslim women to work there. Through her work, Omar fights for religious freedom. The hero works on laws that protect people's rights.

ILHAN OMAR

James Madison

USA 22
James Madison 1809-1817

JAMES MADISON

JAMES MADISON

As part of the Bill of Rights, every American has freedom of religion. Creating the Bill of Rights was a feat of courage. James Madison was a politician who believed in religious freedom. Other politicians did not want a Bill of Rights. They thought it was not important. But this hero stood up for it. He wrote the bill's items. Because of his work, freedom of religion and speech are protected.

CHAPTER 6
EXPANDING HORIZONS

Scientists and explorers are brave. They face many dangers and risks in their work. But they make discoveries. Everyone benefits from their courage.

When Galileo Galilei was born, church leaders were in charge. Their beliefs were law. People who disagreed were often jailed. Some were put to death. This was in the 1500s in Italy.

Galileo studied the night sky. Using math, he formed new ideas. Some were about how the planets moved. This scientist had the courage to share an idea. It was that Earth circles the sun. Leaders did not like this. They said he was wrong. The **astronomer** stood by his ideas. But he was arrested for them. For the rest of his life, he could not leave his home. His written works were banned. Much of today's science is based on Galileo's ideas.

GALILEO GALILEI

Hundreds of feet above the ground, Amelia Earhart spent a lot of time alone. She was a pilot who set many flying records. Earhart broke down gender barriers. Women pilots were very rare. People thought women were not as capable as men. This was in the 1920s and 1930s.

AMELIA EARHART

ATLANTIC OCEAN

In 1932, Earhart flew across the Atlantic Ocean alone. It was the first time a woman had done that. Male pilots had respect for her. Earhart also supported other women. She wanted them to try new things. Flying around the world was one of her goals. The trip was dangerous. On July 2, 1937, she disappeared while flying. No one ever found her. But her feats continue to inspire women today.

It was 2:00 a.m. on May 19, 2006. Temperatures were freezing. Wind was howling. Sophia Danenberg stood on top of the world. She was the first African American to summit Mount Everest. This is the highest mountain on Earth. Her trip there was not easy. Most climbers have help on Everest. Other people carry their gear. Helpers plan a path. Danenberg chose to do it all herself.

Close to the summit, Danenberg was sick. Also, her oxygen mask was not working well. It was very dangerous. Many climbers give up in similar situations. But she pushed through. Her feat has encouraged many others to reach for the top.

GPS

Today, explorers use GPS. This stands for global positioning system. It uses math and satellites to tell people where they are. GPS was made by scientists like Dr. Gladys West.

West is a math expert. In 1956, the U.S. Naval Weapons Laboratory hired her. She was the second African American to work there. In the 1970s and 80s, West did important work that led to the first GPS. In 2018, she was added to the Air Force Pioneers Hall of Fame.

THE FARTHEST FIRSTS

-35,800 FEET
Don Walsh and Jacques Piccard reached the bottom of the Pacific Ocean in 1960.

29,000 FEET
In 1953, Tenzing Norgay and Edmund Hillary climbed Mount Everest. The trip took three months.

19,019 MILES
George Meegan walked from South America to Alaska. He started in 1977. The trip ended in 1983. It is the farthest unbroken walk.

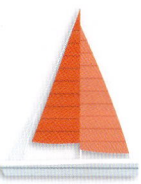

30,123 MILES
Robin Knox-Johnston sailed around the world alone without stopping in 1969. The trip took 10 months.

239,000 MILES
In 1969, Neil Armstrong, Buzz Aldrin, and Michael Collins went to the moon. It was the farthest people had been from Earth.

CHAPTER 7
HEALTH AND SAFETY

Many people have health problems. Others are in accidents. Some have had the courage to then help other people.

Lois Gibbs's family was sick. So were her neighbors. No one knew why. Thankfully, this mother was not going to stay quiet. She had the courage to speak out. Gibbs lived in New York in the 1970s. Years before, chemical **waste** had been buried. It was deep underground.

This hero had to stand up and fight. She talked to her local government. They did not want to fix the problem. But Gibbs got people organized. Together, they kept up the fight. Finally, they won. About 800 families were evacuated. Her feat became famous. Gibbs received 3,000 letters. They came from other families asking for help with waste problems. So she kept working. Her work led to new laws that protect people.

LOIS GIBBS

37

Erin Brockovich stood up to pollution too. This was in the 1990s. A company was making dangerous waste. It got into the drinking water. The company knew what was happening. However, it did not clean up the waste. Many people became ill.

Brockovich began a legal battle. More than a year went by. But Brockovich never gave up. Her team **sued** the company. They won more than $300 million. Most of the money went to help the sick people. In 2000, Brockovich's fight was made into a movie. This feat of courage **empowered** many women.

ERIN BROCKOVICH

In 1980, Candy Lightner lost her daughter. The 13-year-old was killed. A car had hit her. The driver was drunk. The mother turned her grief into action. First, she quit her job. Then, she started a group. It is called MADD. This stands for Mothers Against Drunk Driving. Lightner helped create new laws. New rules were made about drinking and driving. The drinking age was raised to 21.

Alexandra Scott was a brave little girl. She was born in 1996. As a baby, she got cancer. Growing up, she spent a lot of time in hospitals. Doctors helped her. Scott wanted to help them and other kids who were sick. She decided to raise money. With her brother, she started a lemonade stand. The first year, they made $2,000. Every year, they sold lemonade. Eventually they raised more than $1 million. All of the money went to cancer science. In 2004, Scott passed away. A group still raises money in her name.

THE CURIE INSTITUTE

Marie Curie was a scientist. She worked with dangerous radioactive materials. This made Curie sick. She died in 1934, but her research shaped how we fight cancer today.

In the early 1900s, Curie lived in France. She started a center. It is called the Curie Institute. Today, it is a leader in cancer research. Many scientists work there. They discover new treatments. There is a hospital too. People go there for quality care. Curie died so others could be healed.

MARIE CURIE

TIMELINE OF PUBLIC HEALTH CHAMPIONS

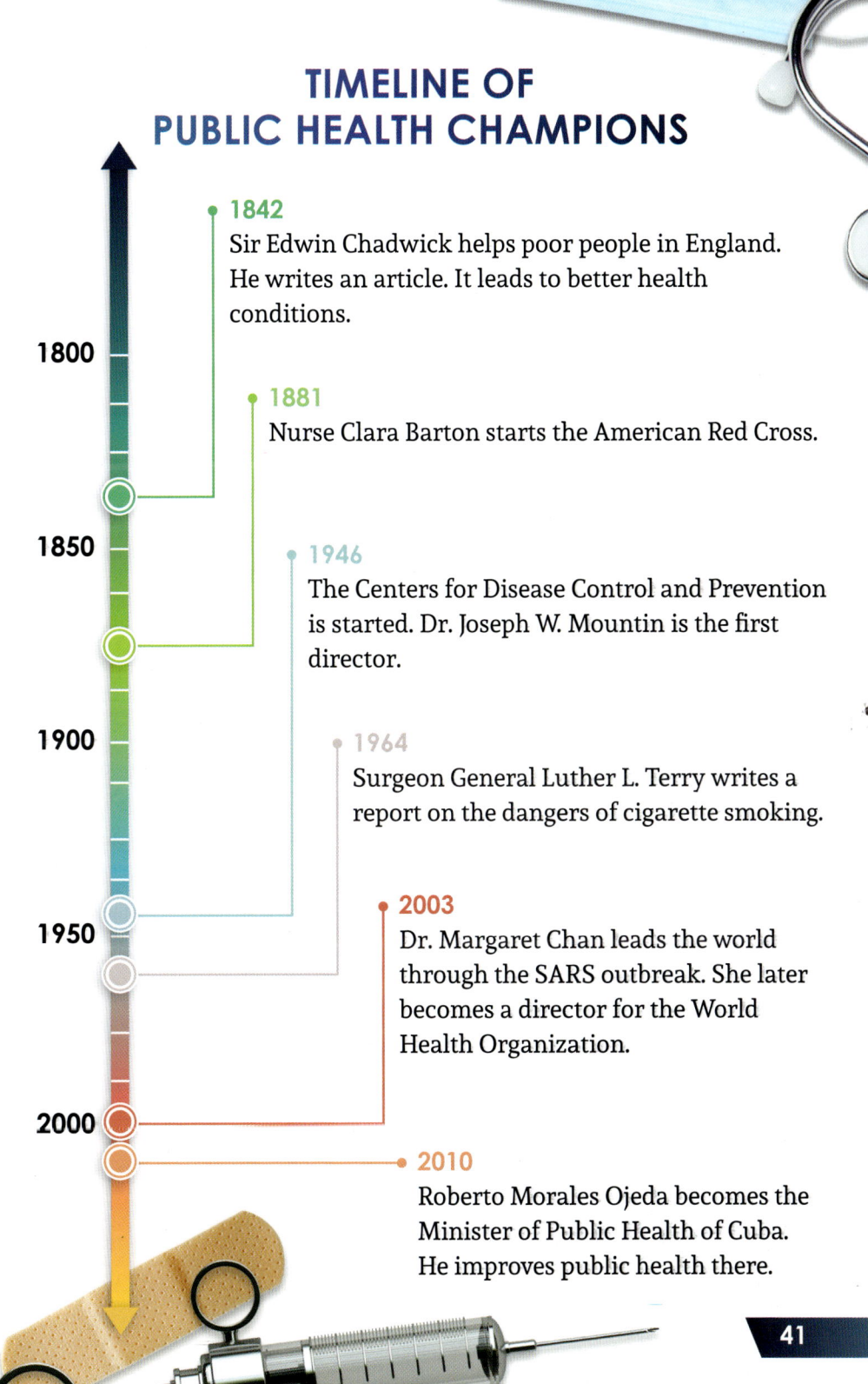

1842
Sir Edwin Chadwick helps poor people in England. He writes an article. It leads to better health conditions.

1800

1881
Nurse Clara Barton starts the American Red Cross.

1850

1946
The Centers for Disease Control and Prevention is started. Dr. Joseph W. Mountin is the first director.

1900

1964
Surgeon General Luther L. Terry writes a report on the dangers of cigarette smoking.

2003
Dr. Margaret Chan leads the world through the SARS outbreak. She later becomes a director for the World Health Organization.

1950

2000

2010
Roberto Morales Ojeda becomes the Minister of Public Health of Cuba. He improves public health there.

CHAPTER 8
DARING RESCUES

Heroes save people in trouble. They face danger in order to help. These rescues are often incredible feats.

Bernard Webber was a member of the U.S. Coast Guard. In 1952, there was a storm. Two boats crashed. Webber took a rescue boat to one. Huge waves smashed the rescue boat. The compass was lost. A searchlight helped the crew find the ship. They loaded the sailors onto the rescue boat. Then Webber took them back to land. More than 30 people were saved. Rescuers were given the Gold Lifesaving Medal. This feat was made into a movie in 2016. It is called *The Finest Hours.*

U.S. COAST GUARD SHIP

It was the morning of September 11, 2001. Two airplanes were flown into the World Trade Center in New York City. Emergency alarms went off. Kevin Pfeifer was a firefighter. His engine answered the alarms. The crew rushed to the North Tower. In the lobby, Pfeifer saw his brother, Joseph. He was a firefighter too. Without much time, the brothers spoke a few words. Then Kevin ran up the stairs. Before long, the building collapsed. Joseph escaped in time. But Kevin did not. He spent his last moments helping other firefighters escape.

JOSEPH PFEIFER

John Volanthen and Richard Stanton are cave divers. They are the best in the world. In 2018, they got phone calls. There was an emergency. A group of Thai soccer players was trapped. The boys were in a cave. It was flooding. Everyone was afraid the boys would drown. The divers were flown to Thailand. There, they did one of the most difficult rescue missions ever. Volanthen and Stanton went 1.5 miles into the cave. This was mostly underwater. Finally, they found the soccer players. Other rescuers were then able to get the boys out.

URBAN SEARCH AND RESCUE

FEMA is a U.S. government agency. It stands for Federal Emergency Management Agency. The agency helps victims of disasters. Special teams are called National Urban Search and Rescue. Crews find people after earthquakes. They rescue people during floods. There are 28 teams. Each team has skilled members. Some are doctors. Others train rescue dogs. These heroes save thousands of people every year.

CHAPTER 9
REBELLION AND REVOLUTION

Freedom was Mahatma Gandhi's dream. He was born in India in 1869. India was ruled by the British. This activist led protests and hunger strikes. In 1930, he led a march. Tens of thousands of people followed him. They marched for 240 miles. It was against the law. Gandhi was arrested. So were 60,000 other people. But the hero kept it up. His country became free in 1947. In 1948, Gandhi was shot and killed. But he had lived to see his dream come true.

Aung San Suu Kyi is from Myanmar. For many years, the military was in charge there. They were often violent and scary. In 1988, Suu Kyi began to speak out. Soldiers put her on house arrest. This means she could not leave her home. She was not completely free until 2010. While there, she worked for peace and freedom. She was given the Nobel Peace Prize. Once she was freed, Suu Kyi joined politics. World leaders met her. Now she works to bring **democracy** to her country.

AUNG SAN SUU KYI

Nelson Mandela was president of South Africa. Before that, he was in prison for 27 years. As a lawyer, he had tried to change laws. White people and black people were kept separate by law. It was called apartheid. Police arrested him for protesting. They almost killed him. Instead, the activist was put in jail for life. In 1990, a new president let him go. Together, the president and Mandela ended apartheid. They won the Nobel Peace Prize in 1993.

It takes courage to stand up to those in charge. These heroes did that. They had a vision for the future. Then they fought for their people.

NELSON MANDELA

TIANANMEN SQUARE

THE UNKNOWN REBEL

In 1989, students were protesting in China. They wanted more freedoms. A large protest was in Tiananmen Square. Soldiers were ordered to shoot and kill. Many tanks arrived. One man stood in front of the tanks. He held up his arm. It made the sign for "stop." The tanks stopped. Then soldiers took the man away.

No one knows the man's name. He is called the Unknown Rebel.

CHAPTER 10
EVERYDAY HEROES

Courage can help everyday people. It enables them to make quick decisions. These choices can save lives.

Jesús García gave up his life to save many others. He worked on a train in the early 1900s. His train went through Mexico. One day, García saw smoke. A train car was on fire. That car had dynamite. He realized it would explode.

There was a town close by. Many people were around. In reverse, García drove the train car out of town. Then the train exploded. The hero died, as well as other workers on the train. But his heroic feat saved many lives. In Mexico, he is remembered as a national hero.

Todd Beamer was on an airplane. He was traveling for work. Suddenly, someone got on the intercom. They had a bomb. Terrorists had taken over the plane. It was September 11, 2001.

FLIGHT 93 NATIONAL MEMORIAL

VERMONT

NEW YORK

MASSACHU

CONNECTICU

TERRORIST TAKEOVER

PENNSYLVANIA

FLIGHT 93 TAKEOFF

OHIO

CRASH SITE

NEW
JERSEY

**PASSENGERS AND
CREW FIGHT BACK**

MARYLAND

WEST
VIRGINIA

DELAWARE

Atlantic
Ocean

VIRGINIA

Beamer and other passengers got together. A vote was taken. Their decision was to fight back. This plane was headed for Washington, D.C. It might have crashed into the White House. No one knows exactly what happened on board. After a fight, the plane crashed in a field in Pennsylvania. Everyone on board died. These courageous people stopped the terrorists.

Felix Ortiz was driving home after school. It was 2019. There was a crashed car upside-down in the road. No police were there. Many people were standing around. Still in the car, the driver was not breathing. Ortiz pulled the driver out. He gave the man **CPR.** After a minute, the man started to breathe again. Police said Ortiz saved his life. The teen said he didn't feel like a hero. Anyone, young or old, can do great things.

Feats of courage can affect just one person. They can also change the world. Heroes may be famous. But they might also be friends or neighbors. No matter what, their courage inspires people to be their best.

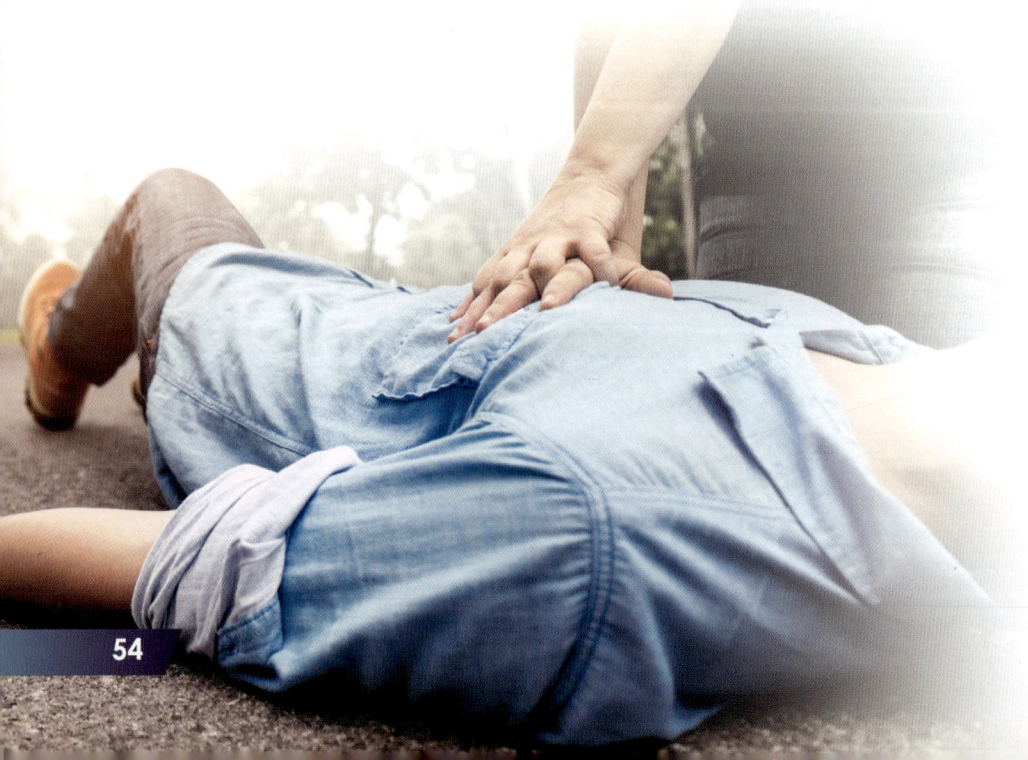

NATURAL DISASTERS

Earthquakes topple buildings. Floods destroy entire towns. Every year, there are natural disasters that put lives at risk. In these emergencies, everyday people can be heroes. They rescue others. Sometimes they save total strangers.

In 2017, there was a hurricane. It was Hurricane Harvey. There were deadly floods. Jacob Cortez was with his family in Texas. He and his father left their house. The heroes went door-to-door. They rescued people from flooding homes. Almost 30 people were saved.

FLOODING FROM HURRICANE HARVEY

GLOSSARY

ACTIVIST
a person who works to create change in politics or society

ASTRONOMER
a person who studies the stars, planets, and space

BOYCOTT
to refuse to take part in an event as a way of protesting

COURAGE
bravery

CPR
a method used to try to save the life of someone who has
stopped breathing; stands for cardiopulmonary resuscitation

DEMOCRACY
a form of government in which people choose leaders by
voting

EMPATHY
the ability to understand and share someone else's feelings

EMPOWER
to make someone stronger or more confident

FEMINIST
a person who believes in equal rights for women

GRENADE
a small bomb that can be thrown or shot from a gun

HEROINE
a woman admired for her courage

MINORITY
a small group of people who are different from the larger group of people that live in a particular area

PROTEST
to speak out or demonstrate against something you disagree with

SCANDALOUS
shocking; outrageous

SEGREGATION
enforced separation of racial groups

SUE
take legal action against someone

SUPREME COURT
the highest court in the U.S.

TRAGEDY
an event that causes great sadness

TRANSLATE
to change words from one language into another

WASTE
unwanted leftover material; trash

WRONGLY ACCUSED

CHAPTER 7

FINGERPRINTS AND BLOOD SPATTER

Fingerprints are used as evidence. So are blood spatter and bite marks. This type of evidence is called pattern or impression evidence. It is left by fingers, blood, or teeth. The patterns are not perfect. False matches can happen.

An elderly woman was killed. A pill bottle was found in the victim's house. The bottle had a fingerprint on it. Detective Dennis Chapman was on the case. He said the print matched Lana Canen. Chapman did not have much training in fingerprints. Canen was convicted.

Years passed. The prints were checked again. A new expert studied them. They did not match Canen's prints. Chapman checked again. He admitted to the mistake. Canen was released. She had spent eight years in prison.

34

35

Wrongful **convictions** happen. Innocent people go to jail. There are many reasons for this. Some people make false confessions. They feel scared. Police might promise a good deal. It may be for less jail time. This can be misleading and confusing.

Forensics can be used incorrectly. Witnesses can also identify the wrong person by mistake.

Other times, criminals lie about a person or an event. These lies can get them less jail time. Sometimes defense lawyers cannot spend much time on cases. They may not be prepared in court.

THE INNOCENCE PROJECT

The Innocence Project helps to free innocent people. It began in 1992. The first project was in New York City. There are now branches across the United States. They are in other countries too.

The project focuses on DNA from crime scenes. Innocence Project experts do DNA tests. They compare their results to the DNA of a convicted person. If there is no match, the person can be proven innocent. This method has freed more than 360 people.

Adults can be wrongly convicted. But it happens to young people more often. Teens may not know their legal rights. A child can also be easily influenced. Young people are three times more likely than adults to make a false confession.

No one knows how big the problem is. More than 2,400 innocent people have been freed in the past 30 years. Each person lost part of their lives. Many other innocent people are never freed.

In 2002, Eric Blackmon was hosting a party. A murder happened at the same time. There was a lineup. One witness picked Blackmon. Another did not.

Blackmon's lawyer made many mistakes. He did not bring alibis to the trial. Blackmon's mother tried to help. She found witnesses from the party. The lawyer did not prepare them. They did not do well in court. Blackmon was found guilty and went to prison.

In prison, Blackmon studied law and worked to free himself. New lawyers were hired. After more than 13 years in prison, he was freed.

GROUP EXONERATIONS

Many convictions can be thrown out at once. This is called a group exoneration. Sometimes a pattern of bad police work is found. Police may want to close a case quickly, so they plant evidence to frame an innocent person. Between 1989 and 2018, group exonerations freed at least 2,500 people. At least 17 different police groups were involved.

CITY	YEARS OF EXONERATIONS	NUMBER OF EXONERATIONS	TYPE OF CHARGES	REASON FOR EXONERATIONS
Philadelphia, PA	2013-2016	1,116 (ongoing)	Mostly drug charges	Misconduct from seven narcotics officers
Philadelphia, PA	1993-1995	360	Mostly drug charges	Misconduct from five officers
Baltimore, MD	2017-ongoing	130 (ongoing)	Mostly drug charges	Gun Trace Task Force misconduct
Camden, NJ	2010-2012	193	Mostly drug charges	Misconduct from five officers
Los Angeles, CA	1999-2000	156	Mostly drug and gun charges	Misconduct from officers in the Rampart division of the LA Police Department

FOR MORE TITLES AND INFORMATION ⟶

space∞ ™

BUSINESS LEADERS

9781680217513

ENGINEERING WONDERS

9781680217575

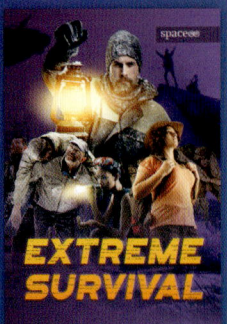

EXTREME SURVIVAL

9781680217483

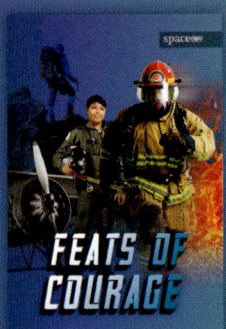

FEATS OF COURAGE

9781680217476

HACKING FOR GOOD

9781680217469

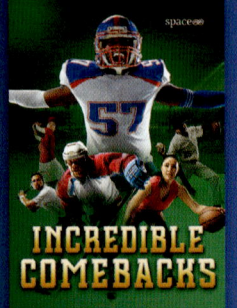

INCREDIBLE COMEBACKS

9781680217490

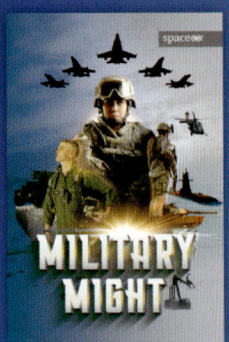

MILITARY MIGHT

9781680217520

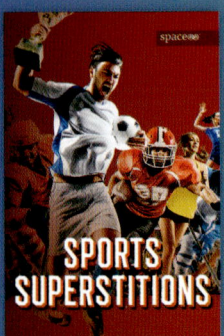

SPORTS SUPERSTITIONS

9781680217445

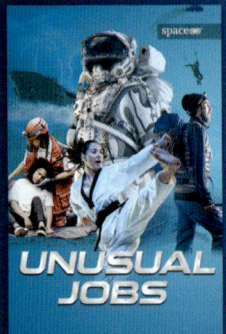

UNUSUAL JOBS

9781680217568

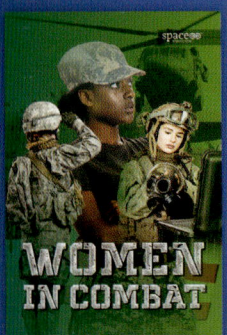

WOMEN IN COMBAT

9781680217506

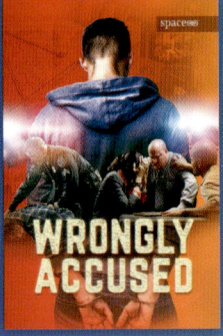

WRONGLY ACCUSED

9781680217452

MORE TITLES COMING SOON

sdlback.com/Space-8